chart hits of 2004

piano
vocal
guitar

ISBN 0-634-07417-2

HAL•LEONARD®
CORPORATION

7777 W. BLUEMOUND RD. P.O. BOX 13819 MILWAUKEE, WI 53213

Visit Hal Leonard Online at
www.halleonard.com

THE VOICE WITHIN
RECORDED BY CHRISTINA AGUILERA
WORDS AND MUSIC BY CHRISTINA AGUILERA AND GLEN BALLARD

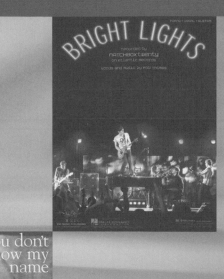

BRIGHT LIGHTS
Recorded by MATCHBOX TWENTY
on Atlantic Records
Words and Music by Rob Thomas

you don't know my name
Recorded by alicia keys
on J Records
Words and Music by
Alicia Keys, Kanye Omari West,
Harold Spencer Lilly,
J.R. Bailey and Mel Kent

SO YESTERDAY
Hilary Duff

SEND YOUR LOVE
RECORDED BY Sting
on A&M Records

Rain on Me
ASHANTI

Me Against the Music
RECORDED BY BRITNEY SPEARS
FEATURING MADONNA ON Jive Records
Words and Music by
Terius Nash, Christopher Stewart,
Dobran Harrickett, Gary O'Brien, Britney Spears
and Thabiso Nkhereanye

crazy in love
Recorded by Beyoncé
featuring Jay-Z on Music World Records
Words and music by
Rich Harrison, Shawn Carter
and Beyoncé Knowles

contents

INDEXED

BRIGHT LIGHTS

Words and Music by
ROB THOMAS

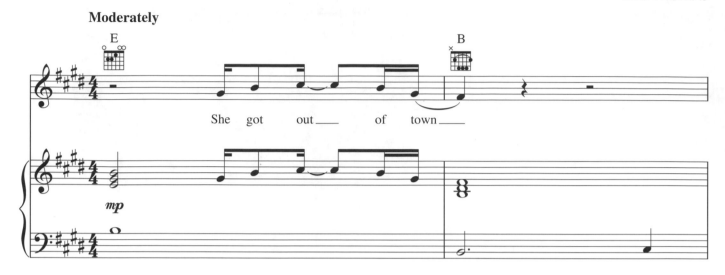

She got out ___ of town ___

on a rail - way New York ___ bound. ___

Took all ex - cept ___ my name, ___

all I'm up a- gainst_ out_ in_ this world?_ And

may - be, may - be, may - be you'll_ find some-thin' that's e -nough to keep_ you. But if the

bright lights don't re - ceive_ you,_ you should turn your-self a - round_ and come on home._

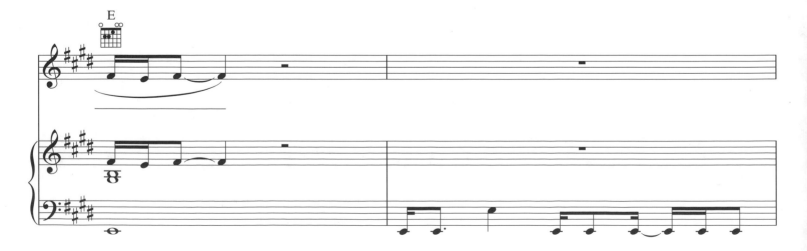

some things in this world, man they don't make sense.

Some things you don't need un-til they leave you. Then the things that you miss, you say....

Ba-by, ba-by, ba-by when all your love is gone, who will save me from

all I'm up a-gainst out in this world? And

To Coda ⊕

may - be, may - be, may - be you'll_ find some-thing that's e -nough to keep_ you. But if the

bright lights don't re - ceive_ you,_ you should turn your-self a -round_ and come on home._

_ Let that cit - y take_ you in._ Come on home._

_ Let that cit - y spit_ you out._ Come on home._

Let that cit-y take___ you down,_____ yeah.___

For God's sake,___ turn a-round.___

Guitar solo ad lib.

D.S. al Coda

Solo ends

CRAZY IN LOVE

Words and Music by RICH HARRISON,
SHAWN CARTER and BEYONCE KNOWLES

Moderate Hip Hop

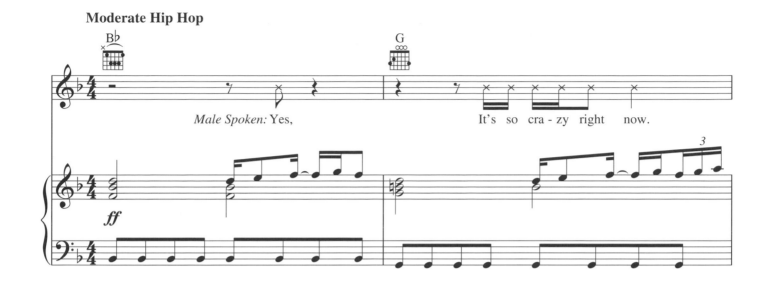

Uh - oh, uh - oh, uh, oh, oh, no - no. Uh - oh, uh - oh, uh - oh, oh, no - no. *Rap ends*

Got me look - in' __ so cra - zy, __ my ba - by. __ I'm not my - self __ late - ly. I'm

fool - ish, __ I don't do this. __ I've been play - in' my - self. __ Ba - by,

I don't __ care. __ 'Cause your __ love's __ got the best of me. __ And ba - by you're mak -

Additional Lyrics

Rap: Young Hov, y'all know when the flow is loco.
Young B and the R-O-C, uh-oh.
Ol' G, big homey, the one and only.
Stick bony, but the pocket is fat like Tony Soprano.
The ROC handle like Van Axel.
I shake phonies, man, you can't get next to the genuine article, I do not sing low.
I sling though, if anything I bling yo'.
A star like Ringo, roar like a gringo.
Bret if you're crazy, bring your whole set.
Jay-Z in the range, crazy and deranged.
They can't figure him out, they like "Hey, is he insane?"
Yes sir, I'm cut from a different cloth.
My texture is the best fur chinchilla.
I been healin' the chain smokers.
How you think I got the name Hova?
I been realer, the game's over.
Fall back young, ever since the label changed over to platinum the game's been a wrap, one.

CALLING ALL ANGELS

Words and Music by PAT MONAHAN,
SCOTT UNDERWOOD, JAMES STAFFORD
and CHARLIE COLIN

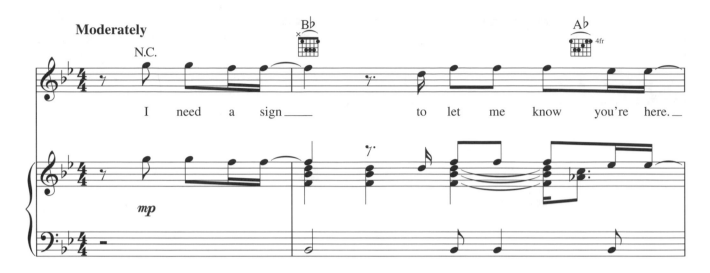

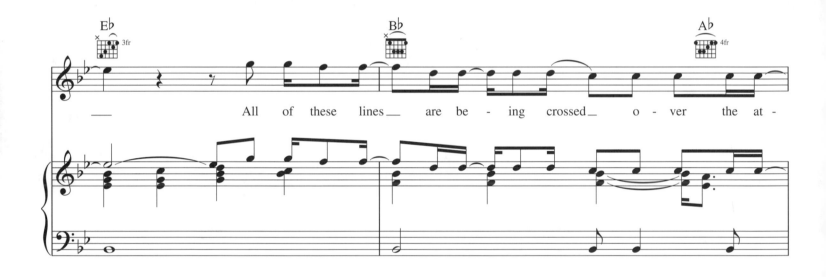

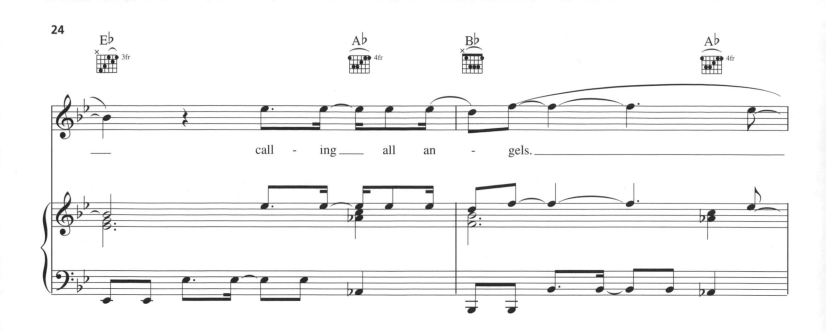

call - ing___ all an - gels.___

And I'm___

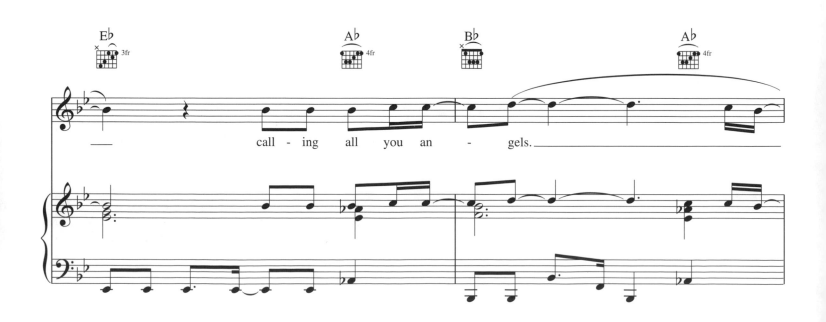

call - ing all you an - gels.___

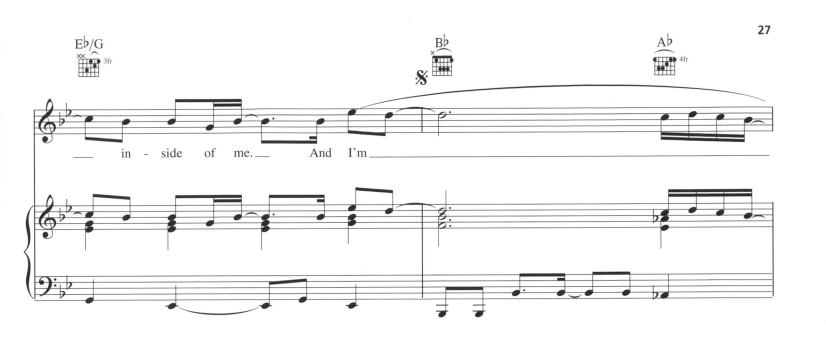

in - side of me.___ And I'm___

call - ing___ all an - gels.___

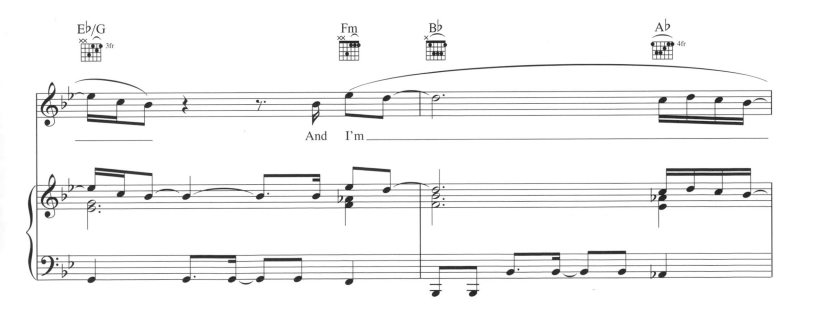

And I'm___

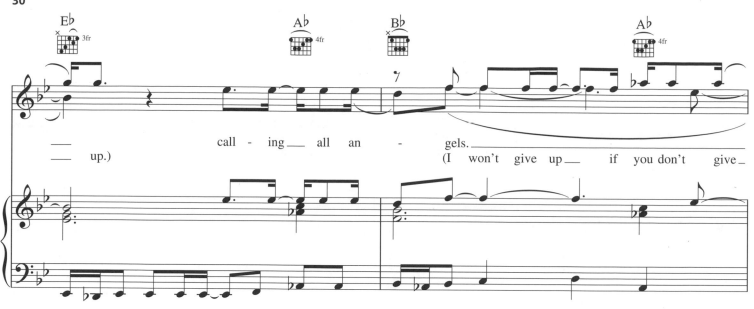

call - ing ___ all an - gels. ___ (I won't give up ___ if you don't give ___
up.)

And I'm ___ (I won't give up ___ if you don't give ___
up.)

call - ing all you an - gels. ___ (I won't give up ___ if you don't give ___
up.)

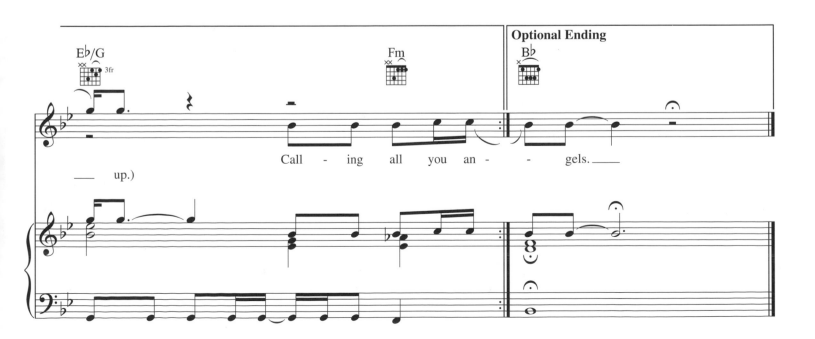

DANCE WITH MY FATHER

Words by LUTHER VANDROSS
and RICHARD MARX
Music by LUTHER VANDROSS

Back when I was a child, be-fore life re-moved all the in-no-cence, my fa-ther would lift me high and dance with my moth-

34

D.S. al Coda

that he would be gone from me. If

Some-times I'd lis-ten out-side her door

and I'd hear how my moth-er cried for him.

I pray for her e-ven more than me. I pray for her e-ven more

DRIFT AWAY

Words and Music by
MENTOR WILLIAMS

FALLEN

Words and Music by
SARAH McLACHLAN

Moderately slow

Heav-en, bend_ to take_ my hand_ and lead me through the fire._ Be the
Heav-en, bend_ to take_ my hand,_ I've no-where left to turn._ I'm

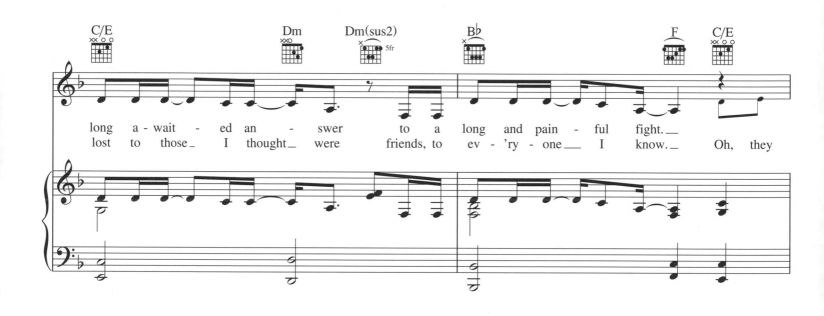

long a-wait-ed an-swer to a long and pain-ful fight._
lost to those_ I thought_ were friends, to ev-'ry-one_ I know._ Oh, they

Truth be told, I've tried_ my best,_ but some-where a-long_ the way_ I
turn their heads, em-bar-rassed,_ pre-tend_ that they_ don't see,_ but it's

To Coda

so don't ___ come ___ 'round here and tell me I ___ told ___ you so. ___

We

all be-gin ___ with good ___ in-tent. Love was raw ___ and young. ___ We be-

lieved that we ___ could change ___ our-selves, ___ the past can be un-done. ___ But we

car - ry on__ our back__ the bur - den time__ al - ways__ re - veals__ in the

lone - ly light__ of morn - ing, in the wound that would__ not heal.__ It's the

bit - ter taste__ of los - ing ev - 'ry - thing__ that I've__ held so__ dear.__

__ I've__ fall - en. I__ have sunk__ so__ low.__

oh, _____ I've _ messed _ up. Bet - ter _ I _ should _ know,

so don't _ come _ 'round here and tell me I _ told _ you so, _____

HARDER TO BREATHE

Words and Music by JAMES VALENTINE,
ADAM LEVINE, JESSE CARMICHAEL,
RYAN DUSICK and MICKEY MADDEN

Moderate Rock

How dare you say that my be-hav-ior's un-ac-cept-a-ble, so con-de-scend-ing, un-nec-

es-sar-i-ly crit-i-cal. I have the ten-den-cy of get-ting ver-y phys-i-cal,

so watch your step 'cause if I do you'll need a mir-a-cle. You drain me dry and make me
What you are do-ing is screw

-er and hard- er to breathe?_ *Guitar solo ad lib.*

Solo ends And does it kill,___ does it burn,__ is it pain - ful to learn___ that it's me___

INTUITION

Words and Music by JEWEL KILCHER
and LESTER A. MENDEZ

Moderate Dance Groove

La di da da. La di da da. La di da da, la la.

I'm just a sim-ple girl___ in a high-tech dig-i-tal world.___

LOOK THROUGH MY EYES

from Walt Disney Pictures' BROTHER BEAR

Words and Music by
PHIL COLLINS

Original key: D major. This edition has been transposed down one whole step to be more playable.

There will be times on this jour - ney,

all you'll see is dark - ness.

through___ my___ eyes._____ Ev - 'ry - thing chang - es.

You'll be a - mazed what you'll find.__ Oh,

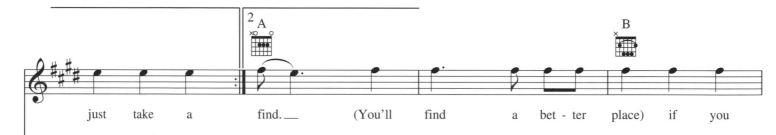

just take a find.__ (You'll find a bet - ter place) if you

look through my___ eyes. (You know there's a bet - ter place.) Just take a

INVISIBLE

Words and Music by DESMOND CHILD,
CHRISTOPHER BRAIDE and ANDREAS CARLSSON

ME AGAINST THE MUSIC

Words and Music by TERIUS NASH, CHRISTOPHER STEWART,
DORIAN HARDNETT, GARY O'BRIEN, BRITNEY SPEARS,
THABISO NKHEREANYE and MADONNA CICCONE

Moderate Dance beat

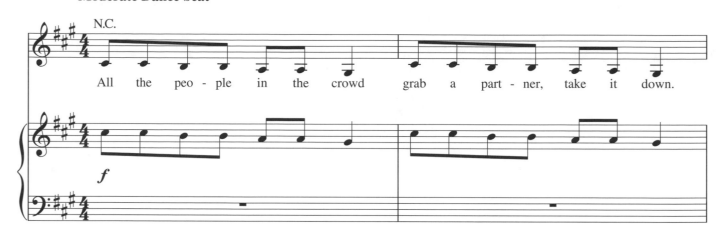

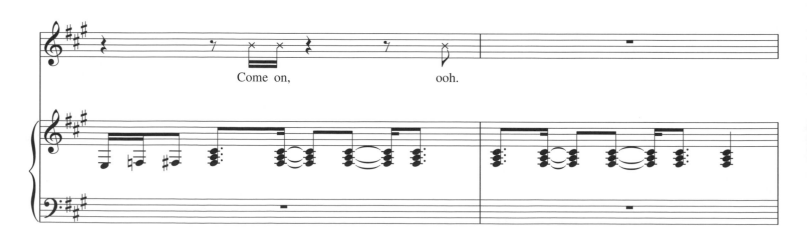

let me see you dance. I wan-na see ya. All my peo-ple in the crowd,

let me see you dance. Come on Brit-ney, take it down. Make the mu-sic dance.

All my peo-ple round and round, par-ty all night long.

Come on Brit-ney, lose con-trol. Grab a part-ner, take it down.

MISS INDEPENDENT

Words and Music by CHRISTINA AGUILERA, RHETT LAWRENCE,
MATTHEW MORRIS and KELLY CLARKSON

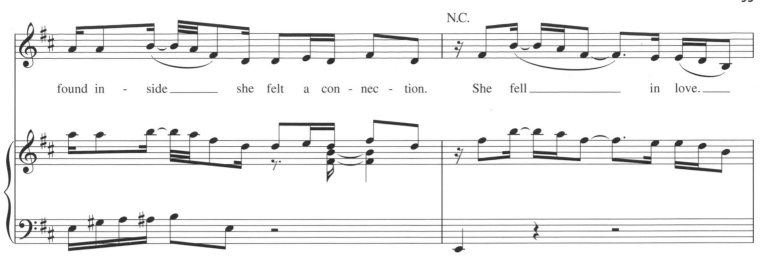

found in - side _____ she felt a con - nec - tion. She fell _____ in love. _____

What is this feel - in' tak - in' o - ver? Think-in' no one could o - pen the door.

Sur - prise, _ it's time _____ to feel _ what's real. _____

THE REMEDY
(I Won't Worry)

Words and Music by GRAHAM EDWARDS,
SCOTT SPOCK, LAUREN CHRISTY
and JASON MRAZ

Well I ___ saw fire-
Well I ___ heard two_

RAIN ON ME

Words and Music by BURT BACHARACH,
HAL DAVID, ANDRE PARKER,
IRVING LORENZO and ASHANTI DOUGLAS

Original key: E♭ minor. This edition has been transposed up one half-step to be more playable.

SEND YOUR LOVE

Music and Lyrics by
STING

Moderate Dance beat

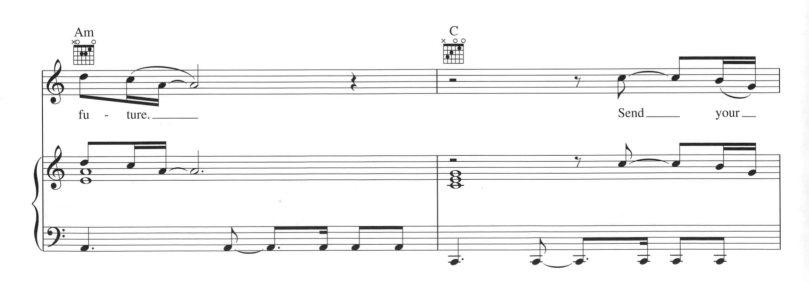

love

into the dis - tant

dawn.

In - side your mind is a re - lay sta - tion. A mis-sion probe in - to the un - known.

SO YESTERDAY

Words and Music by GRAHAM EDWARDS,
SCOTT SPOCK, LAUREN CHRISTY
and CHARLIE MIDNIGHT

Moderate Rock

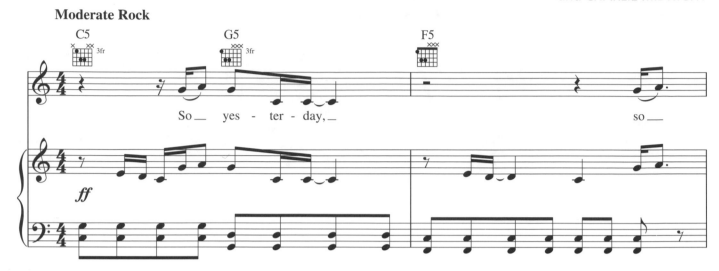

So __ yes - ter - day, __ so __

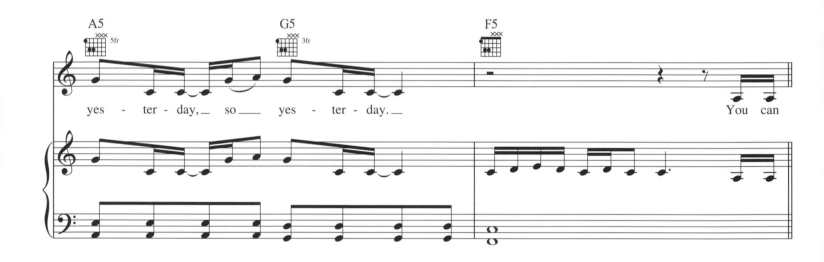

yes - ter - day, __ so __ yes - ter - day. __ You can

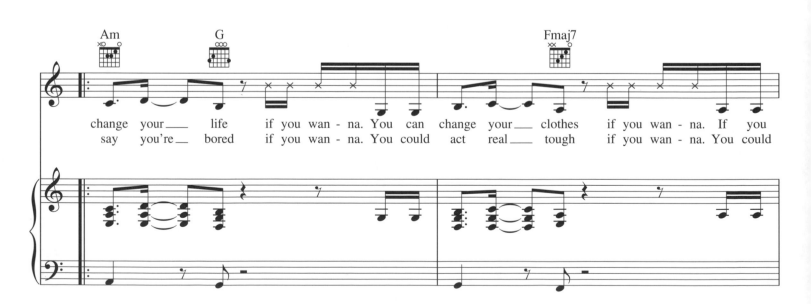

change your __ life if you wan - na. You can change your __ clothes if you wan - na. If you

say you're __ bored if you wan - na. You could act real __ tough if you wan - na. You could

THIS IS THE NIGHT

Words and Music by GARY BURR,
ALDO NOVA and CHRISTOPHER BRAIDE

Moderate Rock

When the world was-n't up - side down, ___ I could

take all the time ___ I had. ___ But I'm not gon - na wait ___ when a mo -

- ment can van - ish so fast. ___ 'Cause

WHITE FLAG

Words and Music by RICK NOWELS,
ROLLO ARMSTRONG and DIDO ARMSTRONG

I know you think that I should-n't still love you, I'll
I know I left too much mess and de-struc-tion to come

tell you that. ___
back a-gain. ___

But if I did-n't say it, well,
And I caused noth-ing but trou-ble; I

I'd still have felt it. Where's the sense ___ in that? ___
un-der-stand if you can't talk to me ___ a-gain.

THE VOICE WITHIN

Words and Music by CHRISTINA AGUILERA
and GLEN BALLARD

find the strength___ that will guide_____ your way___ if you'll learn___ to be-gin_____ to

trust the voice with - in._____

Young girl, don't cry;___ I'll be_____ right here___ when your___ world starts to fall.___

Ooh,_____

mm._____

WHAT DREAMS ARE MADE OF
(Ballad Version)
from Walt Disney Pictures' THE LIZZIE McGUIRE MOVIE

Music by MATTHEW WILDER
Lyrics by DEAN PITCHFORD

Moderately slow, in 2

With pedal throughout

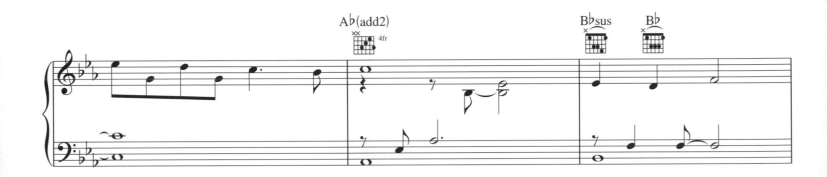

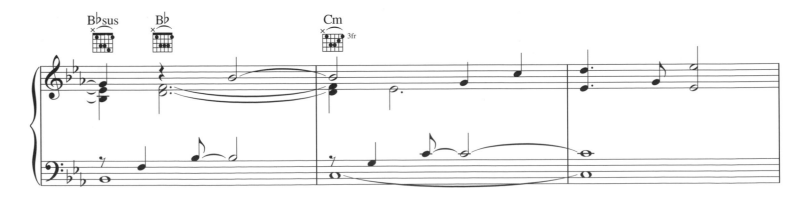

*Male and female vocals both written at sounding pitch

WHY CAN'T I?

Words and Music by LIZ PHAIR,
GRAHAM EDWARDS, SCOTT SPOCK
and LAUREN CHRISTY

Original key: B major. This edition has been transposed down one half-step to be more playable.

YOU RAISE ME UP

Words and Music by BRENDAN GRAHAM
and ROLF LOVLAND

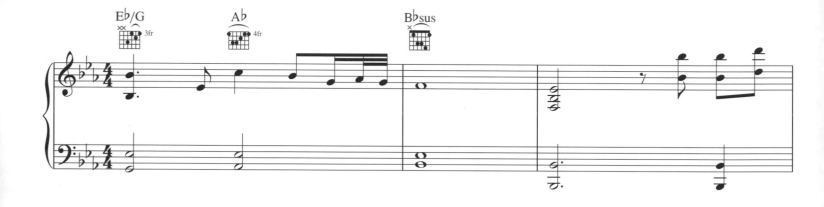

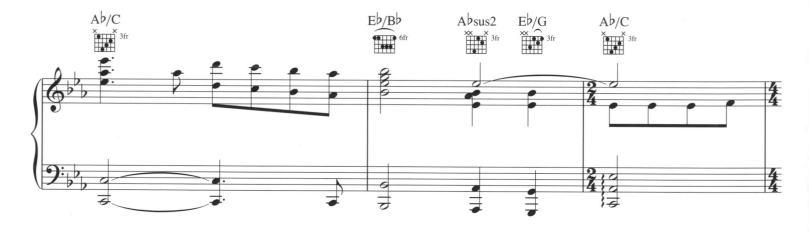

YOU DON'T KNOW MY NAME

Words and Music by ALICIA KEYS,
KANYE OMARI WEST, HAROLD SPENCER LILLY,
J.R. BAILEY, MEL KENT and KEN WILLIAMS

Moderately

Ba - by, ba - by, ba - by, __ from the day I saw you __
Ba - by, ba - by, ba - by, __ I see us on our first date, __

I real - ly real - ly want to catch __ your eye. __
you do - in' ev - 'ry - thing to make __ me smile. __

There's some - thing spe - cial 'bout you. __ I must real - ly like you, __
And when we had our first kiss, __ hap - pened on a Thurs - day, __

Ooh, _____

Spoken: It's funny, he don't even know what he's doin' to me.

ooh. _____

I been feelin' all crazy inside. I'm feelin' like.......

Oh,

do - in' a thing I've nev - er done___ for an - y - one's___ at - ten - tion. Take

no - tice of what's in front of you___ 'cause did I men - tion you're 'bout to miss a good thing?

Spoken Lyrics

I might have to just go ahead and call this boy.
Hello, can I speak to, to, Michael? Oh, hey, how you doin'?
Uh, I feel kinda silly doin' this but um, this is the waitress from the coffee house on 39th and Lenox.
You know, the one with the braids. Yeah, well I see you on Wednesdays all the time.
You come in every Wednesday on your lunch break, I think, and you always order the special with the hot chocolate.
My manager be trippin' and stuff talkin' 'bout we gotta use water but I always use some milk and cream for you 'cause,
I think you're kinda sweet.
Anyway, you always got on some fly, blue suit, mmm.
Your cuff links are shinin' all bright. So what you do?
Oh, word. Yeah that's interesting.
Look man, I mean I don't wanna waste your time but I know girls don't usually do this.
But I was wonderin' if maybe we could get together outside the restaurant one day?
You know, 'cause I do look a lot different outside my work clothes.
I mean, we could just go across the street to the park right here.
Wait, hold up, my - my cell phone breakin' up.
Can you hear me now? Yeah, so what day did you say?
Oh, Thursday's perfect.

Contemporary Classics

Your favorite songs for piano, voice and guitar.

The Definitive Rock 'n' Roll Collection

A classic collection of the best songs from the early rock 'n' roll years – 1955-1966. 97 songs, including: Barbara Ann • Chantilly Lace • Dream Lover • Duke of Earl • Earth Angel • Great Balls of Fire • Louie, Louie • Rock Around the Clock • Ruby Baby • Runaway • (Seven Little Girls) Sitting in the Back Seat • Stay • Surfin' U.S.A. • Wild Thing • Woolly Bully • and more.
00490195 ....$29.95

The Big Book of Rock

78 of rock's biggest hits, including: Addicted to Love • American Pie • Born to Be Wild • Cold As Ice • Dust in the Wind • Free Bird • Goodbye Yellow Brick Road • Groovin' • Hey Jude • I Love Rock 'N' Roll • Lay Down Sally • Layla • Livin' on a Prayer • Louie Louie • Maggie May • Me and Bobby McGee • Monday, Monday • Owner of a Lonely Heart • Shout • Walk This Way • We Didn't Start the Fire • You Really Got Me • and more.
00311566..$19.95

Big Book of Movie Music

Features 73 classic songs from 72 movies: Beauty and the Beast • Change the World • Eye of the Tiger • I Finally Found Someone • The John Dunbar Theme • Somewhere in Time • Stayin' Alive • Take My Breath Away • Unchained Melody • The Way You Look Tonight • You've Got a Friend in Me • Zorro's Theme • more.
00311582 ....$19.95

The Best Rock Songs Ever

70 of the best rock songs from yesterday and today, including: All Day and All of the Night • All Shook Up • Blue Suede Shoes • Born to Be Wild • Boys Are Back in Town • Every Breath You Take • Faith • Free Bird • Hey Jude • I Still Haven't Found What I'm Looking For • Livin' on a Prayer • Lola • Louie Louie • Maggie May • Money • (She's) Some Kind of Wonderful • Takin' Care of Business • Walk This Way • We Didn't Start the Beat • We Got the Beat • Wild Thing • more!
00490424 ....$18.95

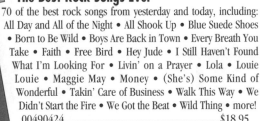

Contemporary Vocal Groups

This exciting new collection includes 35 huge hits by 18 of today's best vocal groups, including 98 Degrees, TLC, Destiny's Child, Savage Garden, Boyz II Men, Dixie Chicks, 'N Sync, and more! Songs include: Bills, Bills, Bills • Bug a Boo • Diggin' on You • The Hardest Thing • I'll Make Love to You • In the Still of the Nite (I'll Remember) • Ready to Run • Tearin' Up My Heart • Truly, Madly, Deeply • Waterfalls • Wide Open Spaces • and more.
00310605 ....$14.95

Motown Anthology

This songbook commemorates Motown's 40th Anniversary with 68 songs, background information on this famous record label, and lots of photos. Songs include: ABC • Baby Love • Ben • Dancing in the Street • Easy • For Once in My Life • My Girl • Shop Around • The Tracks of My Tears • War • What's Going On • You Can't Hurry Love • and many more.
00310367 ....$19.95

Best Contemporary Ballads

Includes 35 favorites: And So It Goes • Angel • Beautiful in My Eyes • Don't Know Much • Fields of Gold • Hero • I Will Remember You • Iris • My Heart Will Go On • Tears in Heaven • Valentine • You Were Meant for Me • You'll Be in My Heart • and more.
00310583 ....$16.95

Contemporary Hits

Contains 35 favorites by artists such as Sarah McLachlan, Whitney Houston, 'N Sync, Mariah Carey, Christina Aguilera, Celine Dion, and other top stars. Songs include: Adia • Building a Mystery • The Hardest Thing • I Believe in You and Me • I Drive Myself Crazy • I'll Be • Kiss Me • My Father's Eyes • Reflection • Smooth • Torn • and more!
00310589..$16.95

Jock Rock Hits

32 stadium-shaking favorites, including: Another One Bites the Dust • The Boys Are Back in Town • Freeze-Frame • Gonna Make You Sweat (Everybody Dance Now) • I Got You (I Feel Good) • Na Na Hey Hey Kiss Him Goodbye • Rock & Roll – Part II (The Hey Song) • Shout • Tequila • We Are the Champions • We Will Rock You • Whoomp! (There It Is) • Wild Thing • and more.
00310105..$14.95

Rock Ballads

31 sentimental favorites, including: All for Love • Bed of Roses • Dust in the Wind • Everybody Hurts • Right Here Waiting • Tears in Heaven • and more.
00311673..$14.95

FOR MORE INFORMATION, SEE YOUR LOCAL MUSIC DEALER,
OR WRITE TO:

HAL•LEONARD® CORPORATION

7777 W. BLUEMOUND RD. P.O. BOX 13819 MILWAUKEE, WI 53213

Visit Hal Leonard Online at www.halleonard.com

Prices, contents & availability subject to change without notice.

0402

THE POP/ROCK ERA

Hal Leonard is proud to present these fantastic folios that gather the best popular songs from the '50s to today! All books arranged for piano, voice, and guitar.

THE POP/ROCK ERA: THE '50s

54 highlights from the first official decade of the pop/rock revolution, including: All Shook Up • At the Hop • Don't Be Cruel (To a Heart That's True) • Donna • Get a Job • Great Balls of Fire • Hound Dog • It's So Easy • Kansas City • (You've Got) Personality • That'll Be the Day • Why Do Fools Fall in Love • and more.
00310788..$14.95

THE POP/ROCK ERA: THE '60s

52 songs that helped shape the pop/rock era, including: Baby Love • Can't Take My Eyes off of You • Crying • Fun, Fun, Fun • Hey Jude • I Heard It Through the Grapevine • I Think We're Alone Now • Louie, Louie • Mony, Mony • Respect • Stand by Me • Stop! In the Name of Love • Wooly Bully • and more.
00310789..$14.95

THE POP/ROCK ERA: THE '70s

44 of the top songs from the '70s, including: ABC • Baby, I Love Your Way • Bohemian Rhapsody • Don't Cry Out Loud • Fire and Rain • I Love the Night Life • Imagine • Joy to the World • Just My Imagination (Running Away with Me) • The Logical Song • Oye Como Va • Piano Man • Three Times a Lady • We've Only Just Begun • You Are So Beautiful • and more.
00310790..$14.95

THE POP/ROCK ERA: THE '80s

38 top pop hits from the '80s, including: Back in the High Life Again • Centerfold • Every Breath You Take • Eye in the Sky • Higher Love •Summer of '69 • Sweet Dreams (Are Made of This) • Thriller • Time After Time • and more.
0031079..$14.95

THE POP/ROCK ERA: THE '90s

35 hits that shaped pop music in the 1990s, including: All I Wanna Do • Angel • Come to My Window • (Everything I Do) I Do It for You • Fields of Gold • From a Distance • Hard to Handle • Hero • I Will Remember You • Mambo No. 5 (A Little Bit Of...) • My Heart Will Go On (Love Theme from 'Titanic') • Ray of Light • Tears in Heaven • When She Cries • and more.
00310792..$14.95

Prices, contents and availability subject to change without notice.

HISTORY OF ROCK

THE HISTORY OF ROCK: THE BIRTH OF ROCK AND ROLL

The first volume explores rock's rhythm and blues roots and its earliest tunes – from "Rocket '88" and "Shake, Rattle and Roll" to the major hits of Elvis Presley, Little Richard, Jerry Lee Lewis, Buddy Holly, and more. 37 songs, including: All Shook Up • Blueberry Hill • Blue Suede Shoes • Earth Angel • Heartbreak Hotel • Long Tall Sally • Lucille • Goodnight, It's Time to Go • The Green Door • Rock Around the Clock • Tutti-Frutti • and more! 136 pages.
00490216 Piano/Vocal/Guitar...................................$12.95

THE HISTORY OF ROCK: THE LATE '50S

The declaration "Rock and Roll Is Here to Stay" led the way for American Bandstand greats like Paul Anka, Frankie Avalon, Fabian, Bobby Darin, and Connie Francis. This book also explores the novelty song hits, the close harmony styles, and romantic ballads that filled the radio waves. 48 songs, including: At the Hop • Chantilly Lace • Do You Want to Dance? • Great Balls of Fire • Lollipop • Rock and Roll Is Here to Stay • Sea of Love • Splish Splash • Tears on My Pillow • Tequila • Wake Up, Little Susie • Yakety Yak • and more. 176 pages.
00490321 Piano/Vocal/Guitar...................................$14.95

THE HISTORY OF ROCK: THE EARLY '60S

Surf music, doo wop, and dance crazes set the stage for a new decade. This volume explores the success of the Beach Boys, "Big Girls Don't Cry," and the Twist. 56 songs, including: Barbara Ann • Breaking Up Is Hard to Do • Do Wah Diddy Diddy • Duke of Earl • Hit the Road, Jack • Louie, Louie • My Boyfriend's Back • Runaway • Sherry • Surfin' U.S.A. • Tell Laura I Love Her • The Twist • Under the Boardwalk • Wooly Bully • and more. 184 pages.
00490322 Piano/Vocal/Guitar...................................$15.95

THE HISTORY OF ROCK: THE MID '60S

The British invaded the charts and Hendrix re-invented the guitar in this volume, featuring chart toppers of the Beatles, the Moody Blues, the Hollies, Rolling Stones, Mamas and the Papas, James Brown, the Byrds, and many more. 49 songs, including: All Day and All of the Night • California Dreamin' • Can't Buy Me Love • Gloria • Groovin' • Help! • Hey Joe • I Want to Hold Your Hand • Wild Thing • Yesterday • and more. 200 pages.
00490581 Piano/Vocal/Guitar...................................$15.95

THE HISTORY OF ROCK: THE LATE '60S

The turbulence of this era created a new mood for rock and roll. From the classic "Sgt. Pepper's Lonely Hearts Club Band" to the San Francisco sound and Janis Joplin to the jazz/rock hits of Blood, Sweat and Tears, you'll find the songs that made the statements of the time in this volume. 47 songs, including: Born to Be Wild • Come Together • Hey Jude • San Francisco (Be Sure to Wear Some Flowers in Your Hair) • Spinning Wheel • The Sunshine of Your Love • White Room • A Whiter Shade of Pale. 190 pages.
00311505 Piano/Vocal/Guitar...................................$15.95

THE HISTORY OF ROCK: THE EARLY '70S

The Beatles broke up, Southern bands brought their brand of rock and roll to the top of the charts, heavy metal was just in its infancy, and "American Pie" glorified the day the music died. Cooper and Bowie made rock a spectacle while the Moody Blues made it an art. From Black Sabbath to Neil Diamond, David Bowie to Elton John, the early '70s were a breeding ground for music superstars still around today. Features 45 hits, including: American Pie • Fire and Rain • Imagine • Maggie May • Rikki Don't Lose That Number • Sweet Home Alabama • and more. 208 pages.
00311538 Piano/Vocal/Guitar...................................$15.95

THE HISTORY OF ROCK: THE LATE '70S

In the late '70s the piano men — Sedaka, John, and Joel — shared the charts with Kansas, Foreigner, and Aerosmith. Women fought for equality and won on the charts with Streisand, Tyler, Ronstadt and Gaynor on top. Underground grumblings of black leather punk began while the music of the Bee Gees and Donna Summer kept people in white satin dancing all night. 43 hits, including: Bad Case of Loving You • Bennie and the Jets • Dust in the Wind • Hot Blooded • I Will Survive • Piano Man • Walk This Way • and more. 208 pages.
00311603 Piano/Vocal/Guitar...................................$15.95

THE HISTORY OF ROCK: THE EARLY '80S

The last dregs of disco were cleaned off the charts by new wave, punk, contemporary hit radio, and heavy metal. The rock heavyweights — John Lennon, Paul McCartney, Stevie Wonder, Chicago, Billy Joel — shared the charts with slick new-comers — Human League, Culture Club, Eurythmics, Police — and the women of rock — Tina Turner, Joan Jett, Cyndi Lauper, Pat Benatar, and many more. 42 songs, including: Do You Really Want to Hurt Me • Every Breath You Take • I Love Rock 'N' Roll • Maniac • Owner of a Lonely Heart • Sweet Dreams (Are Made of This) • Total Eclipse of the Heart • What's Love Got to Do With It • Woman • and more. 256 pages.
00311619 Piano/Vocal/Guitar...................................$15.95

THE HISTORY OF ROCK: THE LATE '80S

Shut up and dance became the war cry of 80s rock as videos paved the way for glamorous new stars. There were New Kids on the Block, Paula Abdul, Madonna, Bobby Brown, Milli Vanilli, and those who had been around the block: Sting, Foreigner, Beach Boys, James Brown, and Robert Palmer. Mega-stars Michael Jackson, Madonna, Bon Jovi, and U2 shot to the top of the charts as rap started easing its way up to the mainstream. 43 songs, including: Addicted to Love • Careless Whisper • Hangin' Tough • If You Love Somebody Set Them Free • Kokomo • Livin' on a Prayer • My Prerogative • Red, Red Wine • Straight Up • We Didn't Start the Fire • You Give Love a Bad Name • and more. 264 pages.
00311620 Piano/Vocal/Guitar...................................$16.95

THE HISTORY OF ROCK: THE EARLY '90S

The early '90s saw a variety of songs fighting for the top spots every week, from R&B ballads from Whitney and Mariah to new releases from old favorites Sting and Meat Loaf. But the pivotal point was when a little-known band from the Northwest hit the airwaves and video channels with "Smells Like Teen Spirit." After Nirvana, grunge became a household name and flannels were officially back in fashion. This book provides a sampling of over 40 of the top tunes of the era complete with a great essay on the trends and hits of the day. Songs include: All I Wanna Do • All 4 Love • Can You Feel the Love Tonight • Dreamlover • (Everything I Do) I Do It for You • From a Distance • Hard to Handle • Hold My Hand • How Am I Supposed to Live Without You • I'd Do Anything for Love (But I Won't Do That) • If I Ever Lose My Faith in You • More Than Words • Mr. Jones • Right Here, Right Now • Smells like Teen Spirit • Tears in Heaven • Two Princes • and more.
00310866 Piano/Vocal/Guitar...................................$16.95

THE HISTORY OF ROCK: THE LATE '90S

The late '90s brought new releases from old favorites like Clapton and Madonna and fresh faces appeared on the scene like Oasis, Jewel, and Chumbawamba. Swing swung back in fashion and Hanson brought pop back to the charts with "Mmm Bop." But one song sunk all the competition: "My Heart Will Go On" from *Titanic* provided the blockbuster the music world was waiting for. This collection provides 42 of the top hits from that time complete with an extensive summary of the bands and events that made those years special. Songs include: Barely Breathing • Beautiful Stranger • Change the World • Counting Blue Cars • Give Me One Reason • I Will Remember You • Iris • Jump, Jive An' Wail • MMM Bop • My Heart Will Go On (Love Theme from 'Titanic') • Semi-Charmed Life • Smooth • Torn • Tubthumping • Wonderwall • You Were Meant for Me • and more.
00310870 Piano/Vocal/Guitar...................................$17.95

FOR MORE INFORMATION, SEE YOUR LOCAL MUSIC DEALER,
OR WRITE TO:

HAL•LEONARD®
CORPORATION
7777 W. BLUEMOUND RD. P.O. BOX 13819 MILWAUKEE, WI 53213

Visit Hal Leonard Online at **www.halleonard.com**

Prices, contents and availability subject to change without notice.